They Worked Together

By Anna Prokos

CELEBRATION PRESS
Pearson Learning Group

Contents

Introduction

Have you ever worked with a partner? Partners are people who work together to get something done. Working with other people can make a job easier and more fun.

Many great events in history took teamwork. This book tells about three teams of partners. Each team worked together to reach its goal.

Edmund Hillary and Tenzing Norgay

Edmund Hillary was born in Auckland, New Zealand, in 1919. When he was sixteen, he took a school trip to the mountains. It was then that he became interested in mountain climbing. As he grew up, Edmund climbed many mountains in New Zealand and around the world.

Edmund Hillary born 1919

Tenzing Norgay was born in Nepal in 1914. Norgay was an expert mountain climber from the Sherpa community. Sherpas are people who live in the foothills of the Himalayan Mountain range. Norgay climbed the many mountains that surrounded his home, and he often helped as a guide on trips.

Tenzing Norgay
1914–1986

China
Nepal
India
N

Mount Everest is in the Himalayan Mountain range.

Edmund and Norgay had the same goal. They both wanted to reach the summit of Mount Everest. It is the world's tallest mountain. Separately both men had climbed the mountain before, but they had never reached the top. In 1953 Edmund and Norgay conquered the mountain together.

Climbing Mount Everest was extremely dangerous. Teamwork helped both men remain safe during their journey. At one point Edmund jumped across a gap in the ice and landed heavily. A huge block of ice broke away. The ice went tumbling down the mountain, and Edmund fell off the edge.

Norgay held onto the rope that was tied to Edmund's waist. He held on with all his might. If he had not done so, Edmund would have been lost forever.

Edmund and Norgay climbed Mount Everest for seven weeks. On May 29, 1953, they reached the summit. Together they were the first people to reach the mountain's peak.

After the successful climb people often asked the men which one of them had reached the summit first.

"We climbed as a team," they always answered.

Edmund and Norgay near the summit of Mount Everest

For years after their climb Edmund and Norgay continued to work together. They spent time helping the Sherpas build schools and hospitals in Nepal. Both Edmund and Norgay wanted to give something back to the people who had helped them achieve their goal.

◀ Children welcomed Edmund at Sotang School, Nepal.

Norgay and Edmund received medals after their climb. ▶

9

Helen Keller and Anne Sullivan

Helen Keller was born in Tuscumbia, Alabama, in the United States in 1880. When she was just nineteen months old, she became sick with a serious illness. The illness caused her to become blind and deaf.

It was difficult for Helen to communicate with others because she could not see or hear. She became frustrated and often misbehaved. Helen's parents wanted to help her as much as they could.

Helen Keller
1880–1968

United States
Alabama

N

When Helen was six years old, her mother heard about Anne Sullivan. Anne attended the Perkins Institution for the Blind. The head of the school asked Anne to be Helen Keller's teacher.

Anne had never been a teacher before. Still she wanted to work with Helen. So she became Helen's teacher the year after she graduated. Anne knew what it was like to be blind. She had lost most of her eyesight when she was a child.

Perkins Institution for the Blind, Massachusetts ▼

**Anne Sullivan
1866–1936**

Anne showed Helen how to use her hands
to communicate. Helen learned to use sign language.
Because Helen couldn't see, Anne had to sign letters
in the palm of Helen's hand. Soon Helen was
signing herself.

With Anne's help Helen also learned to read and write. At first Helen used raised letters, and later she learned Braille. Helen even learned to speak. Eventually Anne went to school with Helen. Anne listened to the teachers. Then she spelled what they were saying into Helen's hand.

Helen finished college when she was twenty-four years old.

Braille

People who can't see can learn to read Braille. In Braille bumps on paper stand for letters. People use their fingertips to read the Braille.

In college Helen began to write a book
about her life. She called it *The Story of My Life*.
Helen wrote many books over the years.

Helen and Anne helped other people, too. Anne showed others how to teach blind and deaf people. Helen let blind people know that they, too, could achieve their goals. As a team they helped raise money for the blind.

Anne Sullivan and Helen Keller became role models for blind and deaf people. They were also admired by others. Their lives and their work touched many people.

Children crowd around Helen during a visit to Melbourne, Australia, in 1948.

Meriwether Lewis, William Clark, and Sacagawea

In 1803 people in the United States had not explored much of the land in the far western part of North America. At this time the United States only extended as far as the Rocky Mountains. People knew the Pacific Ocean was somewhere farther west, but there was no route to get there.

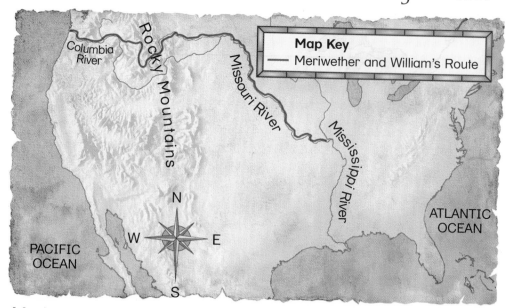

Map Key
— Meriwether and William's Route

Meriwether Lewis and William Clark journeyed west toward the Pacific Ocean.

Meriwether Lewis
1774–1809

William Clark
1770–1838

President Thomas Jefferson asked a former army captain, Meriwether Lewis, to lead a trip to explore the West. Meriwether knew many things about plants and animals. Meriwether asked William Clark to be his partner. William was a wonderful mapmaker, but the job ahead of them was difficult. Neither man knew the land or the Native Americans who lived there.

Meriwether and William needed help on their journey. They were lucky to find a young Native American woman and her family, including her baby son. Her name was Sacagawea (sah-KAH-gah-wee-ah). She knew about the land and was able to communicate with Native Americans along the way.

Like this woman, Sacagawea probably carried her son on her back.

Sacagawea about 1786–1812

Sacagawea, who was only about sixteen years old, led the team across mountains. She found plants to eat when they ran out of food. She talked with the Native Americans they met along the way. Sacagawea also helped get horses and food when the team needed them.

Sacagawea was smart and brave.
Once her boat almost tipped over.
She quickly saved important papers
and supplies that would have been lost.

Sacagawea saved Meriwether and
William from trouble many times. To thank
Sacagawea for her help, William and
Meriwether named a river Sacagawea River.

Meriwether, William, and Sacagawea worked together to help their group travel across thousands of miles. Meriwether and William took notes and made drawings and maps. They crossed rivers and mountains. It was a long, difficult journey.

Once Meriwether was chased by a bear.

When their long trip ended in 1806, the partners
never forgot each other. After Sacagawea died,
William took care of her son, Jean Baptiste.
Meriwether, William, and Sacagawea played
an important part in the history of the United States
and in each other's lives.

This memorial to Meriwether, William, and Sacagawea
is in Montana.

Afterword

Working together is not always easy. Edmund Hillary and Tenzing Norgay had to push each other to keep going. Helen Keller and Anne Sullivan needed patience with one another. Meriwether Lewis, William Clark, and Sacagawea faced the challenges of exploring the unknown.

What did these partners have in common? They never gave up! Partners work hard to reach their goals—together.

Index